Assis dos Santos Meireles
Andrécia Pereira da Costa
Juliete da Silva Souza

Analysis of radio and fiber optic technologies

Assis dos Santos Meireles
Andrécia Pereira da Costa
Juliete da Silva Souza

Analysis of radio and fiber optic technologies

In the quilombola community of Umarizal - Baião

ScienciaScripts

Imprint

Any brand names and product names mentioned in this book are subject to trademark, brand or patent protection and are trademarks or registered trademarks of their respective holders. The use of brand names, product names, common names, trade names, product descriptions etc. even without a particular marking in this work is in no way to be construed to mean that such names may be regarded as unrestricted in respect of trademark and brand protection legislation and could thus be used by anyone.

Cover image: www.ingimage.com

This book is a translation from the original published under ISBN 978-620-6-75671-2.

Publisher:
Sciencia Scripts
is a trademark of
Dodo Books Indian Ocean Ltd. and OmniScriptum S.R.L publishing group

120 High Road, East Finchley, London, N2 9ED, United Kingdom
Str. Armeneasca 28/1, office 1, Chisinau MD-2012, Republic of Moldova, Europe
Printed at: see last page
ISBN: 978-620-7-85099-0

ACKNOWLEDGMENTS

I thank God, who is the light of my path, my refuge, my strength, who has enabled me to continue and complete this journey.

To my family who have spared no effort to support me, to my wife Daysiane Rodrigues Meireles, who has always been by my side helping me and contributing as much as possible, to my daughters Cleysiane Rodrigues, Maria Fernanda Meireles and Thayane Meireles, for understanding my absence during my studies.

I would like to thank my parents Manoel Meireles and Maria Osmelita dos Santos for their support during this phase of my academic life, and my siblings who welcomed me into their home. To Alcy Corrêa, who also welcomed me into his home with open arms and shared some of his life experience, helping me to be here today.

To all my friends who helped me directly and indirectly when I needed it, especially Janderson Souza (in memory) who encouraged me to carry on.

To my teachers for their dedication, for sharing learning and knowledge that I will carry with me for the rest of my life, especially Dr. Otávio Noura Teixeira, Dr. Daniel da Conceição Pinheiro, Dr. Renato Luiz Cavalcante and Dr. Caio Carvalho Moreira.

To my advisor, Professor Dr. Andrécia Pereira da Costa, and to my co-supervisor, Professor Juliete da Silva Souza, thank you for your trust in my work, for your respect, and for helping me whenever I came to you.

To the board members Professor Dr. Otávio Noura Teixeira and Professor Dra. Thamyris da Silva Evangelista for her willingness to evaluate my work.

I would like to thank my quilombola community of Umarizal, Baião-PA, where I was born, grew up and currently live, and which made it possible for me to enter this higher education course through the PSE, thank you all very much.

SUMMARY

2

This paper discusses radio and fiber optic technologies in the quilombola community of Umarizal. The research addresses the two technologies present in the community's internet provider Conect_A&D. The general objective was to analyze the radio and fiber optic technologies in operation at the Internet provider in the quilombola community of Umarizal, Baião. This research aimed to obtain comparative data between the two technologies, using a field study methodology with a qualitative approach. To this end, specific applications and *software* were used, among other practical analyses, in order to achieve the general objective of the research. The results obtained reveal the differences between the technologies in terms of speed, stability, costs, advantages and disadvantages. Finally, the results show that despite the fact that fiber optic technology costs twice as much to deploy, it offers a better quality service and larger bandwidths. However, in the community of Umarizal, radio stands out for its ability to serve users where there are no conditions for laying optical cables.

Keywords: Analysis. Comparison. Optical fiber. Internet. Radio.

ABSTRACT

This work discusses radio and fiber optic technologies in the quilombola community of Umarizal. The research addresses the two technologies present in the Conect_A&D internet provider in the community. Thus, the general objective was to analyze the radio and fiber optic technologies that are in operation at the internet provider in the quilombola community of Umarizal, Baião. This research aimed to obtain comparative data between the two technologies, in this sense, the field study methodology was used with a qualitative approach. For this, specific applications and software were used, among other practical analyzes in order to achieve the general objective of the research. The results obtained reveal the differences between the technologies in terms of speed, stability, costs, advantages and disadvantages. Finally, the results indicate that despite the high cost being twice as high to implement fiber optic technology, it offers a better quality service and higher bandwidths. However, in the community of Umarizal, the radio route stands out for its ability to serve users where there are no conditions to lay optical cables.

Keywords: Analysis. Comparison. fiber optic. Internet. radio.

LIST OF ABBREVIATIONS AND ACRONYMS

ABRANET   Brazilian Internet Association
ANATELA   National Telecommunications Agency
AP   *Access Point*
BL   Broadband

COVID-19   Coronavirus disease

EPON   *Passive Optical Network*

FTTH   *Fiber to the Home*
GHz   Giga-hertz

GPON   *Gigabit Passive Optical Network*

HOST   Host

IEEE   *Institute of Electrical and Electronic Engineers*

IP   *Internet Protocol*

ISP   Internet Service Provider

ITU-T   *International Telecommunication Union*

Optical Line   Terminal

WHO   World Health Organization

ON   Optical Network Terminal
ONU   *Optical Network Unit*

PING   *Packet Internet Network Grouper*

PPOE   *Point-to-Point Protocol over Ethernet*

PPP   *Point-to-Point Protocol*
PTP   *Point-to-Point*

RB   *Routerboard*

               SCMS Multimedia Communication Service

SFP   *Small Form Factor Pluggable*

SLIP   *Serial Line Internet Protocol*

TCP   Transmission Control Protocol

ICT   Information and Communication Technology

WLAN   *Wireless Local Area Network*

1   INTRODUCTION

The world has undergone transformations over the years in many ways and the internet is a milestone that has changed people's way of life. The internet "is a computer network that connects thousands of devices around the world" (KUROSE, 2013). It is a system made up of a set of logical protocols, structured on a global scale for public and unrestricted use, with the aim of enabling data communication between terminals via different networks (BRASIL, 2014).

According to Macedo *et al.* (2018), a computer network consists of a set of autonomous and interconnected devices for the purpose of exchanging data through a single technology.

In the specific case of the Internet, communication takes place through a specific language or protocol, called TCP/IP (*Transmission Control Protocol/ Internet Protocol*), which reads the information transmitted and sends it to the destination established by the user (OLIVEIRA, 2007).

Since the popularization of the Internet for domestic purposes, the number of users has gradually increased. According to Internet World Stats[1] , in April 2022, there were five billion Internet users worldwide, which represents 63% of the global population.

With the emergence of the Covid-19 virus, declared by the World Health Organization (WHO) in March 2020, preventive measures were determined, such as social distancing and isolation, with which people could not go out to work, study, walk, among other daily tasks.

In the face of what has happened, digital technologies have played a fundamental role in continuing the activities interrupted by the Covid-19 virus, which are now carried out remotely, depending directly on the internet. Information technology was one of the great differentials in the pandemic context, serving as a way of disseminating information, used by all segments of society, the government and other entities (DAVI; OLIVEIRA, 2007).

The internet has been essential for digital devices such as cell phones and computers located in different places to be able to communicate. Today's society is living through a great era of globalization, which is increasingly connected through

---

[1] "Internet World Stats - Usage and Population Statistics." https://www.internetworldstats.com/. Accessed July 21, 2022.

the use of the internet. During the pandemic, this scenario became even more widespread, making the current moment a major milestone in modern society (BEAUNOYER; DUPÉRÉ; GUITTON, 2020).

In Brazil, a survey carried out by NIC.br[2] in April 2022 revealed the habits of internet users during the pandemic in 2021. According to the study, during the pandemic, 99% of Brazilian users used their cell phones to access the internet. The study also found that 94% of Brazilian households have internet access. In addition, Brazilians have carried out various activities on the internet, including: buying products and services *online, online* public services, remote learning and work. And around 89% of users watch videos, programs, films or series online.

With more people connected to the internet and using different digital platforms at the same time, the demand for broadband internet (BL) has increased. According to a survey carried out by the National Telecommunications Agency (ANATEL), broadband internet gained more than 5 million subscribers in 2021 in Brazil, a 14% increase in the number of accesses, jumping from 36.3 million registered users in December 2020 to 41.4 million identified in 2019. Broadband internet is characterized by transmitting internet at high speed and stability, meeting the demands of users.

> High-speed broadband is seen internationally as a key element for economic development. As well as opening up the possibility of more access to information, culture and education, it is essential for increasing productivity, creating better quality jobs and diversifying the economy (MACHADO, 2017).

In large urban centers, broadband internet access is available on mobile devices through 3G, 4G and 5G technology provided by the country's major telephone operators, but this is not the case in many towns far from the major urban centers. This is the case of the quilombola community of Umarizal, in the rural area of Baião – PA, where this type of technology is not available, and broadband internet access is possible through ISPs (*Internet Service Providers*) that provide fixed broadband.

> The fixed broadband service, called Multimedia Communication Service (SCM) by the National Telecommunications Agency (Anatel),

---

2 "In the Media - The impact of the pandemic on Internet use - NIC.br." 7 Apr. 2022, https://www.nic.br/noticia/na- midia/cyber-cultura-o-impacto-da-pandemia-no-uso-da-internet/. Accessed July 26, 2022.

seeks to meet consumer needs related to leisure, distance education, research, teleworking, visualization, creation and sharing of content, through the online consumption of texts (news), audios, videos, and a series of other functionalities. (ANDRADE, 2023)

In this pandemic context, ISPs have established themselves as an alternative for providing fixed broadband services, using radio or fiber optic technology, playing the role of distributor and interconnector of the world wide web, the Internet, in accordance with ANATEL standards.

Law No. 12.965 of April 23, 2014 (Marco Civil da Internet), which establishes principles, guarantees, rights and duties for the use of the internet in Brazil, has contributed to the regulation and expansion of ISPs. According to cetic.br, in 2021 there were 12,826 Internet providers in Brazil.

Based on the information presented, in the Quilombola Community of Umarizal, in the municipality of Baião/PA, during the period of the covid-19 pandemic, residents also suffered from the preventive actions imposed on society. Unlike urban centers, they were left adrift, as they depended directly on the urban area of the city of Baião for financial and commercial activities. Internally, schools and other services were interrupted, students from the universities UNIFESSPA (Federal University of South and Southeast Pará) and UFPA (Federal University of Pará) returned to the community, the elderly were isolated and residents of other localities were prevented from moving within the territorial limits of the village.

On the other hand, residents have sought alternatives to continue their activities remotely and the internet has contributed to this. It is in this context that the internet provider Conect-A&D, which has been in operation for over 10 years and was a pioneer in setting up and distributing the internet in this community, is the subject of this research.

1.1   Justification

At the start of the pandemic, the Brazilian government and educational institutions had not yet devised a strategy for continuing the activities that had been interrupted. The provider in question supplied internet using radio technology, which met the needs of users during this period.

As the months of 2020 passed, the number of users increased significantly and with the advent of digital remote access platforms such as *Google Meet, Zoom, Microsoft*

Teams, Discord and other technologies, they began to demand more Mbps (megabits per second) of internet. As a result, in order to meet the needs and demands during and after the Covid-19 pandemic, the provider integrated fiber optic technology into its system.

With this in mind, this study aimed to analyze the radio and fiber optic technologies in operation at the Conect_A&D Provider, in order to compare which of the two technologies is more stable, which transmits more data, what the cost-benefit ratio is and in which scenario it is most appropriate to use them, among other practical analyses, since both technologies are important and viable depending on the scenario and location.

1.2   Objectives

1.2.1   General Objective

Analyze the radio and fiber optic technologies that are in operation at the Internet provider in the Quilombola Community of Umarizal, Baião.

1.2.2   Specific objectives

- Introducing the technologies used in the Internet service provider;
- Compare the types of radio and fiber optic technologies;
- Present the advantages and disadvantages;
- Evaluate the cost-benefit ratio;
- Compare the two technologies in practice.

1.3   Structure of Work

As for the structure of the work, the next chapters are as follows: Chapter 2 highlights the theoretical framework of radio and fiber optic technology, as well as the foundation of topologies, network infrastructure and structured cabling. Chapter 3 shows the methodology and definition of network projects and their main communication protocols, the structure of the provider and how it is distributed. Chapter 4 covers the results and discussions of this research, analyzing PING, speed, router channel costs and the advantages and disadvantages of radio and fiber optic technologies.

2   THEORETICAL REFERENCE

This chapter covers the main concepts and characteristics of radio and fiber optic technologies and network topologies.

2.1   Via Radio

The internet via radio is called WLAN (*Wireless Local Area Network*), a local network that uses radio waves to communicate between network equipment. It is among the options most used by small and medium-sized providers to bring connections to remote locations (POSSEBON, 2014). For this technology to reach the end user, it needs a system that allows radio frequency waves to be emitted by antennas installed on towers at strategic points. These waves are picked up by the antenna at the subscriber's home. This equipment picks up the signal sent by the radio tower and transfers it to the router and other electronic devices, called *hosts*, which make it possible to connect to the internet.

Because of the process of transmitting waves from a tower to an antenna, high places without trees or buildings nearby are more suitable for this type of connection. Radio transmission is characterized as follows:

> Radio waves are easy to generate, can travel long distances and easily penetrate buildings; they are therefore widely used for communication, whether indoors or outdoors. Radio waves are also omnidirectional, which means that they travel in all directions from the source; in this way, the transmitter and receiver do not need to be carefully and physically aligned (TANENBAUM, 2011).

Another characteristic for radio signal distribution is the classification of the WLAN network into *outdoor* and *indoor*.

> The network is classified as outdoor when the radio frequency signal is transmitted through free space in outdoor environments, and mostly with a direct and long-range view of the network. An indoor network is a classification given to a network that transmits a radio signal indoors and usually with obstacles (POSSEBON, 2014).

The issue of *outdoors* and *indoors* makes it possible to connect in rural communities, because depending on the environment, WLAN network equipment is configured to operate accordingly. In this context, small internet access providers have gained ground and have become the main means of providing radio telecommunications services in different rural locations in the country and "already lead the market in more than 1,200 municipalities and are responsible for 12% of total connections in the country", according to an analysis by ANATEL, published in 2018.

In a recent survey, this data was evidenced and published by the Abranet (Brazilian Internet Association) website in June 2022 and can be seen in Figure 1.

Figure 1 - Households with internet access, by area (2008-2021).

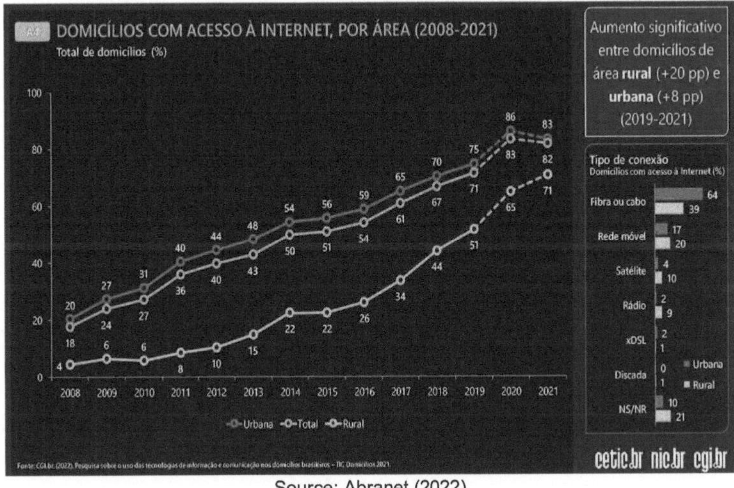

Source: Abranet (2022).

According to research carried out by Abranet, there has been an increase in internet access between 2008 and 2021, with an emphasis on rural areas, which has led providers to invest in an alternative to bring connections to rural areas, which at first opted for radio internet.

2.2   IEEE standard 802.11

As far as equipment is concerned, there is a classification of protocols that are used to standardize devices that use *wireless* networks. The IEEE 802.11 standards are widely used by providers. The IEEE (Institute of Electrical and Electronics Engineers) establishes the standardization of equipment.

This proliferation of standards meant that a computer equipped with a brand X radio wouldn't work in a room equipped with a brand Y base station. Finally, the industry decided that a wireless LAN standard might be a good idea, and so the IEEE committee that standardized wireless LANs was given the task of drawing up a wireless LAN standard. The standard was given the name 118802.11. A common nickname for it is WiFi. It is an important standard and deserves respect, so we will call it by its correct name, 802.11 (TANENBAUM *et al.*, 2011).

The growing demand for faster and more reliable connections has resulted in an advance in the WIFI protocol. As the technology evolved, new standards were developed over time. These include: 802.11a (transmission up to 54 Mbps, operating in the 5.1-5.8 GHz band); 802.11b (transmission up to 11 Mbps, operating in the 2.4-2.485 GHz band) and 802.11g (transmission up to 54 Mbps, operating in the 2.4-2.485 GHz band) (KUROSE; ROSS, 2006).

The latest evolution of the IEEE standard is 802.11n. With a bandwidth of up to 300 Mbps, a range of 70 meters and operating on the 2.4GHz and 5GHz frequencies, which uses several antennas to transfer data from one place to another, its main benefit is the increase in bandwidth and range (RAMOS, 2020).

2.3   Protocol PPPoE

This protocol is used by internet service providers to authenticate clients and guarantee the security of a connection with the internet service provider and the user through an authentication defined for each one, with a username and password. PPPoE establishes the session and authenticates with the ISP. "At the end of the 1980s, the *Serial Line Internet Protocol* (SLIP) was limiting the growth of the Internet. The *Point-to-Point Protocol* (PPP) was created to solve remote connectivity problems with the Internet" (FERNANDES, 2009).

PPPoE (*Point-to-Point Protocol over Ethernet*) is a protocol for connecting users on an Ethernet network to the Internet. The PPPoE protocol derives from the PPP protocol, establishing the session and performing authentication with the Internet access provider (SOARES; MARTINS, 2017).

2.4   Structure of an Internet Service Provider via Radio

The basic equipment for setting up a radio structure is an RB (*RouterBoard*)[3] , Panel or Sectorial[4] , long-range PTP (point-to-point) antennas, network cables, RJ45

---

[3] "Routerboard: a world of possibilities for managing ." 30 Nov. 2020, https://www.dicomp.com.br/noticia/155/routerboard-um-mundo-de-possibilidades-para-gerenciamento-de-networks. Accessed Aug. 12, 2022.
[4] "Sectorial Antennas - Wireless Networks - ConectWi." https://www.conectwi.com.br/redes-wireless/encontre-as- melhores-opcoes-de-antenas-sectoriais-aqui-na-conectwi.html. Accessed August 12,

connectors, service equipment in users' homes, routers and other necessary materials. This structure is mounted on a tower to receive and distribute the[5] internet *link.*

Figure 2 illustrates how the equipment of a radio provider is distributed.

Figure 2 - Radio provider structure.

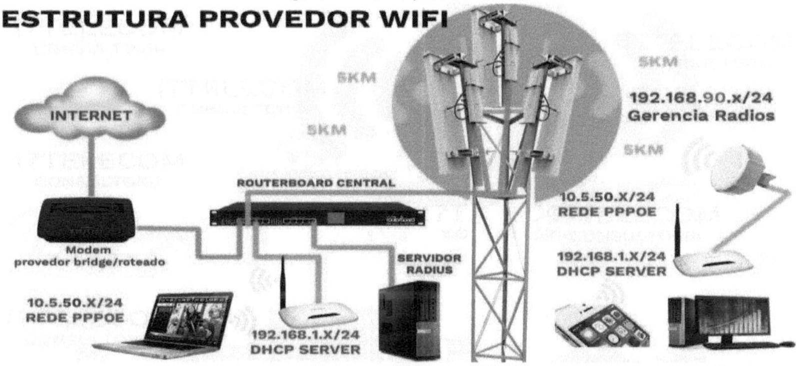

Source: i7telecom (2017).

The entire structure of radio internet depends on where the tower will be installed to receive and transmit the *link*, as this decision will affect the distribution and quality of the service. "Electromagnetic waves propagate in any medium. Earth surface and atmospheric effects affect their propagation, which directly affects the performance of the wave" (POSSEBON, 2014).

2.5 Fiber Optics

Faced with the scenario of high consumption of data packages, fiber optic internet is gaining ground in the technology market due to its speed and better performance in delivering this service. Invented more than 50 years ago, optical fiber is capable of transporting data at the speed of light.

Vieira (2017) says the following about fiber optics:

Conceptually, Optical Fibre is characterized by being an advanced technology that arrives through physical cables that run along the poles until they reach the customer's home or business premises, providing greater stability and reliability with high internet bandwidth rates. Fiber optic cable is considerably faster, lighter and more durable than metal wire media, making it more suitable for systems that require the transfer of large volumes of data.

The cables are made of transparent materials such as glass fibers or plastic and are used as a means of propagating light. "It can carry light over distances ranging from

2022.

[5] "Meaning of Link (What it means, Concept and Definition)." https://www.significados.com.br/link/. Accessed Aug. 12, 2022.

a few centimeters to more than 160 km. Optical fibers operate individually or in bundles. Some single fibers are less than 0.025 mm in diameter" (BERTOZZI, 1994).

Figure 3 shows the encapsulation of fiber optic cable in detail.

Figure 3 - Fiber optic cable.

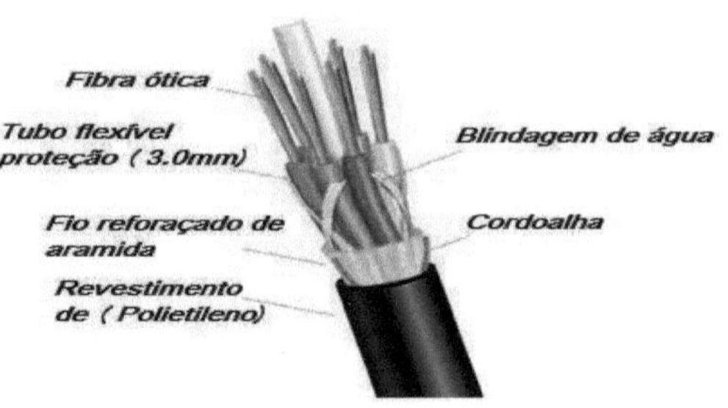

Source: Mauricio (2020)

2.6 Optical networks Passive

A PON network is a point-to-multipoint optical network that enables the sharing of a single optical fiber between several end points (users) (SILVA, 2018).

The passive optical network, or PON, is designed to allow a single fiber from a service provider to maintain an efficient broadband connection for multiple end users. These end users are usually individual customers who use PONs in a commercial environment. PONs are known as high-speed, high-performance networks. In Brazil, this type of technology has been gaining excellent projection due to its characteristics (ARAÚJO, 2019).

Over the years, and with the arrival of new services and applications that require greater bandwidths, the development of PON network architectures has matured, coming up with a new proposal to share the broad bandwidth made available by fiber between different users, using an optical splitter. Services and applications such as cloud computing, video on demand (VoD), videoconferencing, high-resolution image transfer, high definition television (HDTV), among others, are already a reality and the demand for bandwidth continues to grow upwards, both downstream and upstream (RAMOS; NEVES; 2018).

In the passive network, most of the equipment does not need to be connected to the power grid, there are only two points connected to the power grid, which would be the OLT (optical line terminal), this equipment can be found in the central office of the contracted company and the ONU (*Optical Network Unit*), which is allocated inside the customer's home (FREITAS, 2022).

The typical architecture of a PON network containing only passive optical components is shown in Figure 4.

Figure 4 - Typical architecture of a PON network with passive components.

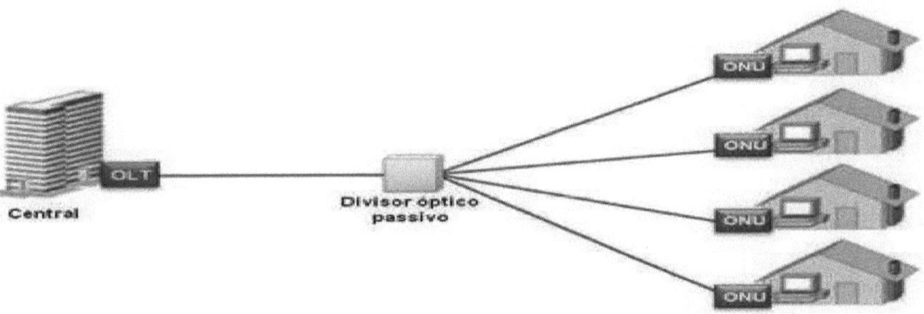

Source: Teleco (2023).

The use of passive elements is the most important feature of PON networks. The term passive comes from the main characteristic of this network, since there are no active elements, i.e. elements that require electrical energy for their operation (PICIN; GIMENEZ, 2015). Depending on the number of customers the service provider will serve, the network can be designed with one of the PON versions (EPON or GPON), as they have different characteristics.

EPON has fractionation rates of 1:16 and 1:32 and works with an average bandwidth per user of 60 and 30 Mbit/s respectively. The organization responsible for EPON is the IEEE and its specifications are defined in IEEE 802.3ah. It provides rates of 1 Gbit/s both downstream using a wavelength of 1490 nm (voice and data) and 1550 nm (video), and upstream using a wavelength of 1310 nm. OLTs in EPON can connect to 16 or 32 ONUs. GPON is a standard defined by the ITU-T, has a split ratio of 1:64 and is expected to use a split ratio o f 1:128 in the advancement of the technologies used, thus being able to obtain greater support according to the evolution in the number of ONTs and ONUs managed by each OLT. (SILVA, 2018)

Figure 5 shows the characteristics of EPON and GPON technology.

Figure 5 - Characteristics of EPON and GPON technologies.

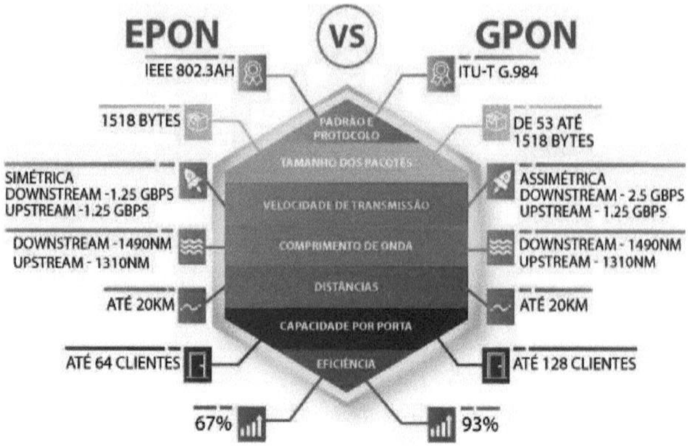

Source: Fibracem (2019).

EPON technology meets the needs of small and medium-sized providers and can serve up to 512 ONUs simultaneously. If this number is exceeded, GPON technology is ideal. Figure 6 shows the network structure with OLT equipment in EPON and GPON versions.

Figure 6 - Network structure with OLT EPON and GPON.

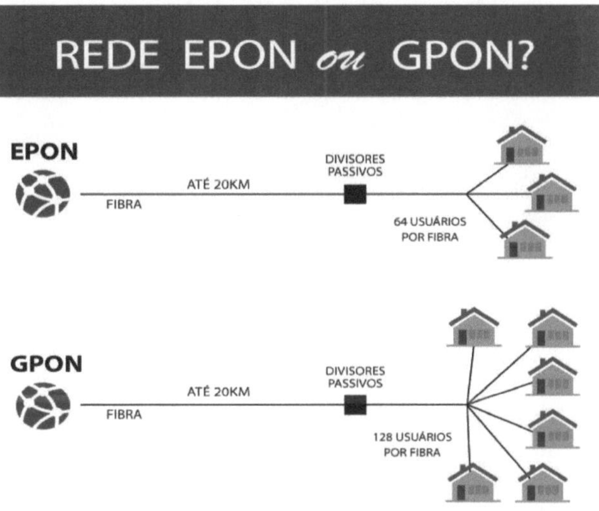

Source: Fibracem (2019).

Starting from the EPON and GPON network structure, the internet provider has two options for investing in fiber optic technology. The feasibility of the choice will be determined by the FTTH (*Fiber to the home*) network project, which involves the implementation of optical fiber throughout the access network, i.e. from the distribution center to the final equipment placed in the customer's home (MENESES FILHO, 2018).

2.7 Fiber Optic Network Project - FTTH

When thinking about a fiber optic network structure, first of all you need a project with a total survey of the area where the main network will be installed and the equipment that will take the internet via fiber to the users. Figure 7 shows the FTTH project drawn up for the community of Umarizal, indicating the quantity of materials needed to implement fiber optic technology, such as optical cable, CTO, CEO and other equipment.

Figure 7 shows a fiber optic network project.

Figure 7 - Project for the implementation of the Fiber Optic Network in the Quilombola Community of

Source: Author (2020).

Once the project is complete, you have a general idea of the types of fibers used to build the FTTH and the entire path it takes from the central equipment station to the user's home (MARTINS, 2008). The purchase of materials becomes more efficient, since you have an overview of the types of equipment needed and the quantity. It is also possible to know which standards and protocols to use and which technology to work with, be it GPON or EPON.

Figure 8 illustrates the main equipment used in a fiber optic network.

Figure 8 - Basic equipment for fiber optic service.

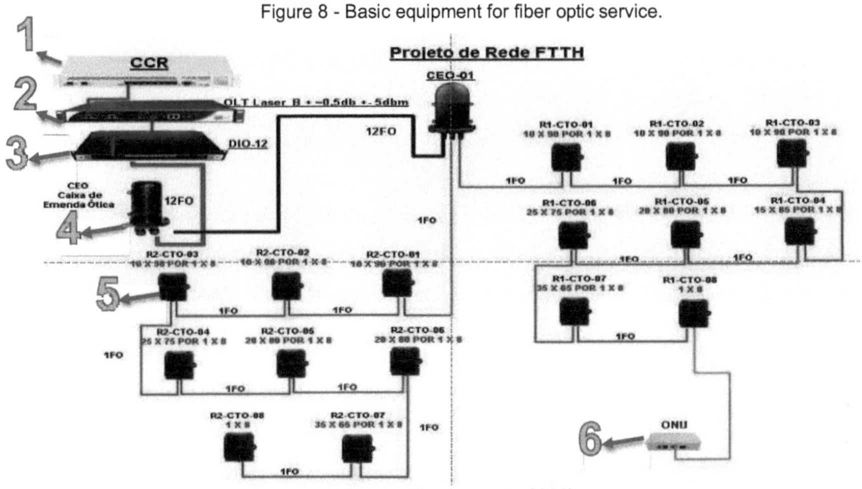

Source: Fscommunit (2020).

Figure 8 shows item 1, a mikrotik ccr device that manages clients such as adding, deleting, bandwidth control and other functions, item 2, an OLT (optical line terminal), is the device responsible for managing and distributing access to data and *streaming* services, *and* item 3, a DIO (optical internal distributor), which accommodates and protects the fusions made between optical cables and optical extensions, allowing the cabling that makes up the structure of a fiber optic network to be organized and stored. The first 3 items are fixed to the server rack. In item 4 we have a CEO (Optical Splice Box) where the splices of the optical cables laid on the poles are accommodated, 5 is a CTO (Optical Termination Box) is used for distribution of drop cable cabling to the end user who will receive internet in the equipment illustrated in item 6 of Figure 8. What determines the type of EPON or GPON technology to be used is the number of customers, the number of *links,* among other factors.

2.8 Topologies of Network

The topology of a computer network can be defined as the way in which the stations (terminal systems) connected to a network are interconnected (STALLINGS, 1997).

2.8.1 Point to point

This type of topology is used to interconnect two devices from one end to the other. They are interconnected directly via a transmission medium. It is a low-cost structure and easy to implement. The problem with this type of topology is poor security and problems with scaling up.

The point-to-point topology can only be used to provide connectivity between two devices or in peer-to-peer communication networks. In some situations, it may be interesting to connect two devices directly to exchange data (MACEDO, 2018). Figure 9 illustrates the point-to-point topology.

Figure 9 - Example of a point-to-point topology.

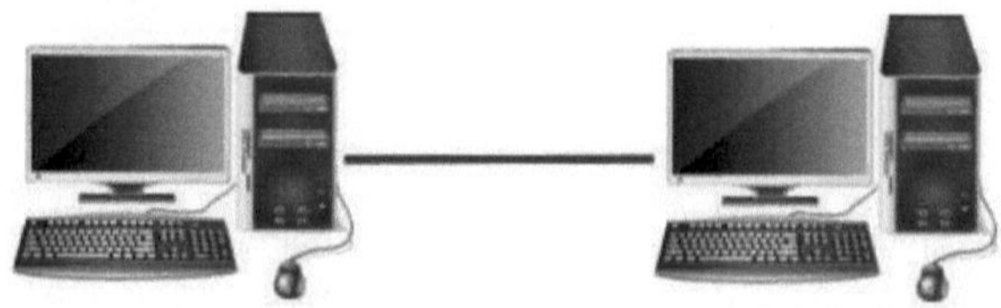

Source: Yuri Matheus (2018).

2.8.2 Bus

In the bus topology, all the devices are connected to a single cable, called the bus, which is a disadvantage because if the main cable has a problem, the whole network is compromised. The advantage is the simplicity of installation, connecting or disconnecting the cable on the bus. The main applications of the physical bus topology are coaxial cable networks, wireless networks and fiber optic networks. Figure 10 shows an example of a bus.

Figure 10 - Example of a bus topology.

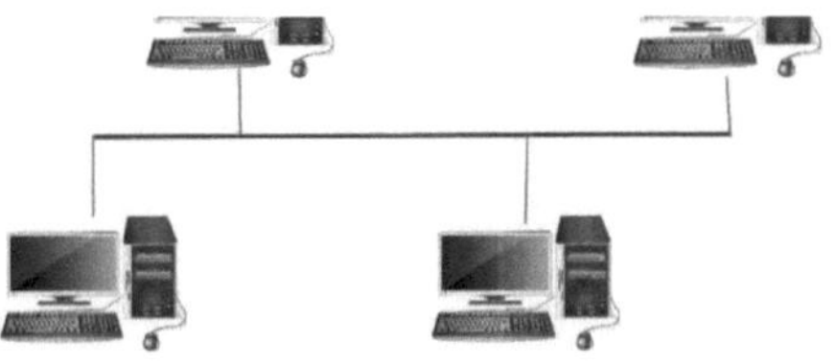

Source: Yuri Matheus (2018).

2.8.3   Ring

In the ring topology, the computers are organized in series, forming a closed circuit. It is a type of computer network in which the devices are connected in a closed circular shape, where each device is connected to its neighbor. One advantage of the ring topology is that it is easy for a message to be delivered to all the other computers on a network. However, the ring topology also has disadvantages in terms of failures and delays in data processing. The links connecting the devices and the network devices themselves are not immune to faults. Figure 11 illustrates the ring topology.

Figure 11 - Example of a ring topology.

Source: Fábio dos Reis (2016).

2.8.4   Star

In this type, all the devices on the network are connected to a single central point, such as a *switch* or *hub*. Whenever a computer wants to send packets to a certain destination, the data must pass through the central node (MACEDO, 2018).

This configuration offers several advantages. Firstly, the star topology makes it easier to manage the network, as each device communicates directly with the central point. This makes it easier to identify and resolve problems. If one device has a problem, the other devices will continue to function normally, since they don't depend on each other to transmit data. Figure 12 illustrates the star topology.

Figure 12 - Example of a star topology.

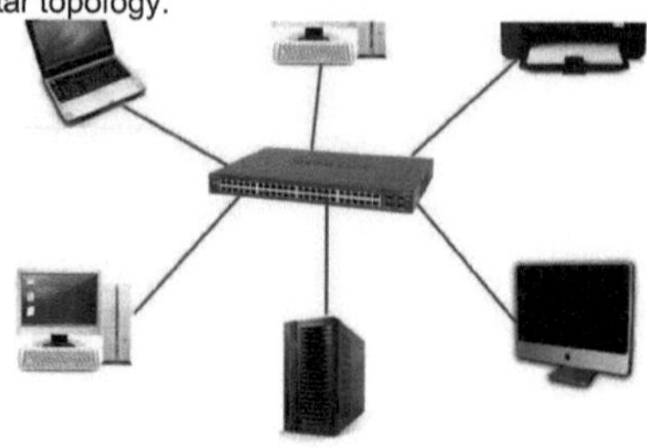

Source: Fábio dos Reis (2016).

This network topology is used in most local area networks (LAN), whether in an office, a home or a university, and has a set of computers that are directly connected to a router, *switch* or *hub* to exchange data (MACEDO, 2018).

2.8.5   Mesh

A computer network organized in a mesh topology has two main properties: the devices can communicate with each other, as long as they are both within reach of each other (MACEDO, 2018). Because the devices communicate with each other, there is less chance of failures; if one fails, it won't harm the others. Figure 13 illustrates the mesh network topology.

Figure 13 - Example of a mesh topology.

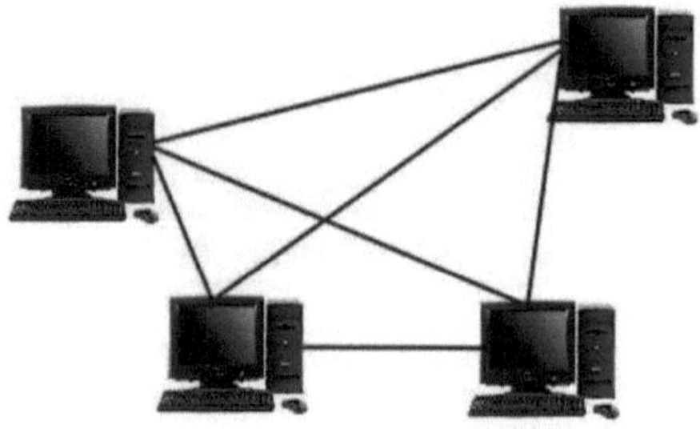

Source: Fábio dos Reis (2016).

2.8.6   Tree

The tree network topology consists of joining other topologies on the same bus. This tree topology is nothing more than a visualization of the interconnection of various networks and subnets (FRANCISCATTO *et al.*, 2014).

It has a central station where the others communicate, the tree format has this characteristic because it contains the central element referred to as the root and the branches at the ends are called leaves. Figure 14 illustrates the tree topology.

Figure 14 - Example of a tree topology.

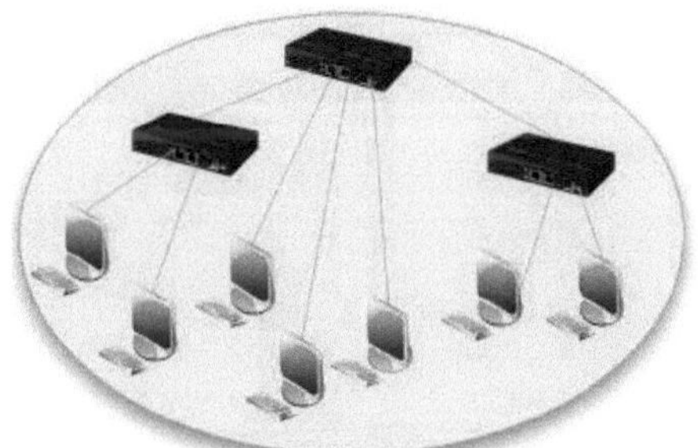

Source: Fábio dos Reis (2016).

2.8.7   Hybrid

The hybrid topology is made up of two or more types and is applied to networks larger than a LAN. It is called a hybrid topology because it can be formed by different types of topology, i.e. it is formed by joining, for example, a bus network and a star network, among others (FRANCISCATTO *et al.*, 2014).

One of the advantages for companies and other organizations is the use of the existing structure in the expansion process using other topologies. It is reliable, supports a large amount of traffic and can be modified according to need. The disadvantages are the complexity of implementing the project, expensive equipment and infrastructure.

Figure 15 shows a hybrid network topology made up of several topologies.

Figure 15 - Example of a hybrid topology.

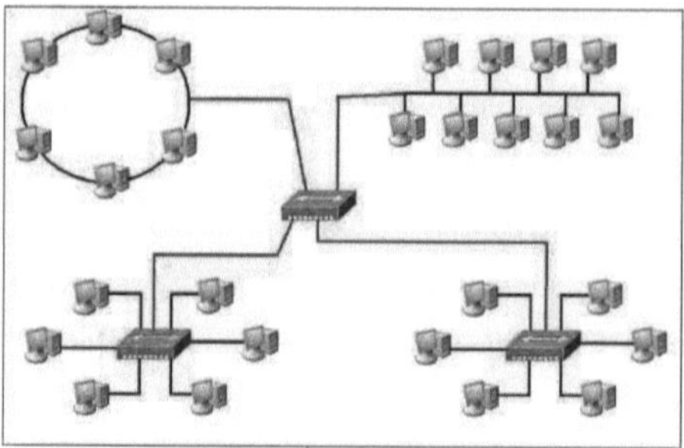

Source: Paulo Neiva (2023).

Among the types of topologies that exist, the provider in the Umarizal community uses a hybrid topology because it is a radio and fiber optic network, both with different physical topological structures.

3 METHODOLOGY

The methodology adopted in this work was a field study. Field research is characterized by investigations in which, in addition to bibliographical and/or documentary research, data is collected from people, using different types of research (ex-post-facto research, action research, participant research, etc.) (FONSECA, 2002). As for the approach, qualitative research was used, using technological resources such as digital tools and applications to measure the quality of radio and fiber optic technologies.

In the qualitative approach, the researcher is not concerned with quantifying the facts, Gerhardt and Silveira (2009) define the following:

> Researchers who use qualitative methods seek to explain why things happen, expressing what should be done, but they don't quantify values and symbolic exchanges, nor do they subject themselves to the test of facts, because the data analyzed is non-metric (elicited and interactional) and uses different approaches.

These methods were used to analyze the two technologies in operation at the internet provider conect-A&D, in the quilombola community of Umarizal-Baião. The research was carried out between 2020 and 2021. The following topics will detail the structure, network layout, distribution, results and discussions, cost analysis, advantages and disadvantages and conclusion.

3.1 Structure of the Internet Service Provider at Umarizal

The Quilombola community of Umarizal, a rural area in the municipality of Baião, is located on the left bank of the Tocantins River and is a Quilombola remnant community with a population of more than 2,500 inhabitants, according to a report carried out by the Umarizal Polo School in 2013.

Figure 16 illustrates the location of Umarizal-Baião where the internet provider is located.

Figure 16 - Location of Umarizal-Baião.

Source: Google Maps (2022).

The locality has an extensive area of large trees and preserved forests. By land, it is 120 km from the city of Tucuruí - PA and 100 km from the city of Cametá - PA. Figure 17 illustrates the Umarizal landscape in more detail.

Figure 17 - Umarizal today.

Source: Huroshi Bogéa (2022).

The community's distance from urban centers was one of the determining factors for the company to choose to provide internet via radio, the other being that at the time the internet provider was set up in the community, fiber optic technology had not yet reached the urban area of Baião and the surrounding towns.

Initially, the entire structure was designed for a radio provider that would serve customers over the radio. Over time, fiber optics became a reality in the municipality, making it possible to distribute internet via fiber.

Although fiber optic internet is available to users, many continue to be served via radio, for two reasons, one by choice and the other due to the lack of electricity poles in certain neighborhoods, since power poles are used to lay optical cables.

3.2 Internet Network Diagram at Umarizal

The internet *link* reaches the PoP of the Umarizal internet provider via two routes, via optical cable and via radio, where the main link 1 used is optical fiber and *link* 2 (via radio) is used in case of *FailOver*. Figure 18 illustrates how the main server is structured with the arrival of the *link* on optical fiber, via radio and redistribution by the two technologies.

Figure 18 - Main server structure.

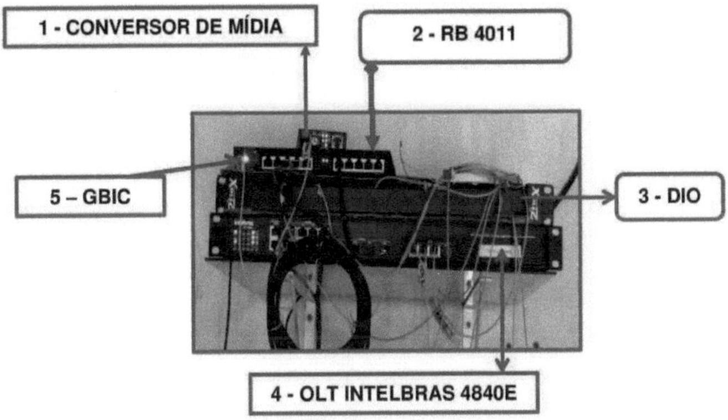

Source: Author (2022)

Figure 18 shows the equipment in the main server structure: (1) media converter which converts the optical light signal to radio frequency; (2) RB (Routerboard) 4011 which manages the provider; (3) DIO (Internal Optical Distributor) is the equipment responsible for providing flexibility and organization to the fiber optic cables, it protects and accommodates fusions between extensions and cables; (4) OLT (optical line terminal) is the equipment responsible for communication between server and client and (5) Gbic, which converts the electrical signal into an optical signal and provides greater flexibility and better network performance.

3.2.1 Distribution

Since setting up the internet in the Umarizal community in 2011, the internet provider has only offered users radio internet. Since 2020, it has offered internet via fiber optics and is in the process of migrating its customers to this new technology.

In order to reconcile the two types of technology, *link* 1 arrives at the Umarizal server via optical cable on BR 422 (Transcametá), while the second *link* arrives at the first 100% fiber AP (Baião) and is converted into radio frequency via the *Mikrotik* radio to be sent *wirelessly* by the Ubiquiti antenna. When the *link* arrives at the second AP (Umarizal), it is received by the same equipment mentioned in the AP (Baião).

With the *link* available at the AP (Umarizal), a fiber optic cable is connected to the SFP port of the *Mikrotik* radio where it converts the radio waves into a light beam to the main management server via the 12FO fiber cable. During the execution of the fiber optic project, two fibers were previously separated, one for the arrival of *link* 1 (radio link), and the other for redistributing and serving radio customers back to the tower.

Figure 19 shows the distribution of the internet provider in operation in the quilombola community of Umarizal. With both radio and fiber optic technologies.

Figure 19 - Distribution of Internet providers in Umarizal.

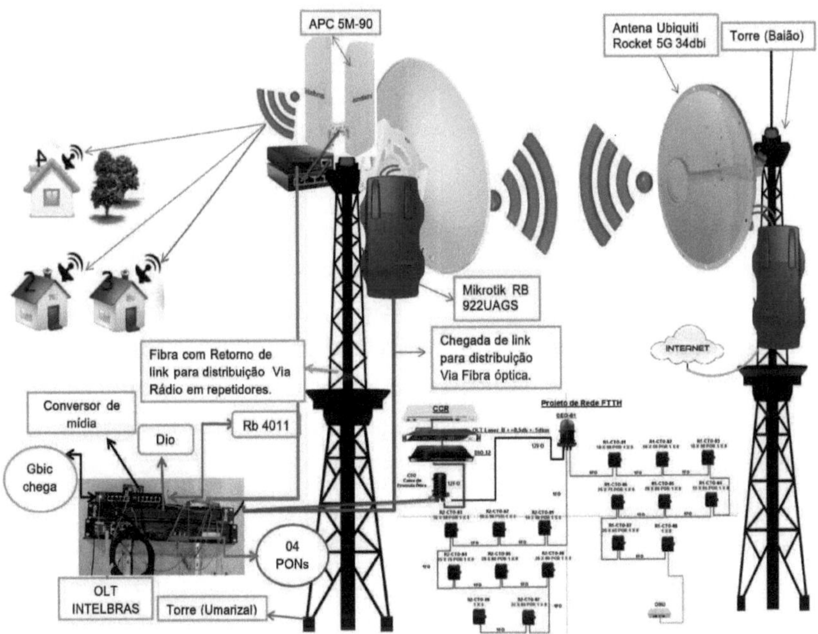

Source: Author (2022).

4   RESULTS AND DISCUSSIONS

This chapter presents the results and discussions of the practical analysis of *ping*, speed, channels, costs and the advantages and disadvantages of radio and fiber optic technologies.

4.1   Ping Analysis Between the Two Technologies

The *Packet Internet Network Groper* (PING) is available on all operating systems. PING is a tool that analyzes the time it takes to send data packets and replies between machines connected to the same network, providing important information such as: first it tells you if the host is available (PING reply) and how long the message takes to come back, the reply is displayed in milliseconds (ms), the shorter this time the better the internet speed, on the other hand, the higher the PING value, the slower the data transmission and the more difficult it is to synchronize information in real time. A high PING shows one of the reasons why the internet connection is slower.

In order to analyze PING between radio and fiber optic internet users, tests were carried out remotely from the PoP to the customer's home. The PoP (*Point of Presence*) is the place where the provider keeps the telecommunications equipment needed to allow its customers to access the internet.

To remotely access Internet users, we used the Winbox application, which is a free utility program created by the MikroTik company. It is a network manager for use with the RouterOS firmware. Its use implies greater control over the stability of routing interfaces. Available for PC, the software has an intuitive interface, making it versatile to use. (Winbox, 2023)

It communicates with the Mikrotik RouterOS device, which makes it possible to manage the device called RB 4011iGs+. Clients are registered on this device and authenticated via PPPOE with a *login* and password. Once the devices have been integrated between provider and client, an IP address is assigned to each one, allowing them to be accessed from the PoP.

Figure 20 shows the customer management equipment.

Figure 20 - Customer management.

Source: Author (2023).

To identify the radio and fiber optic clients, they were named: client A (radio) and client B (fiber optic), and the PING test was carried out using the Mikrotik RouterOS terminal. Figure 21 shows the interface of the Mikrotik terminal.

Figure 21 - mikrotik Terminal interface.

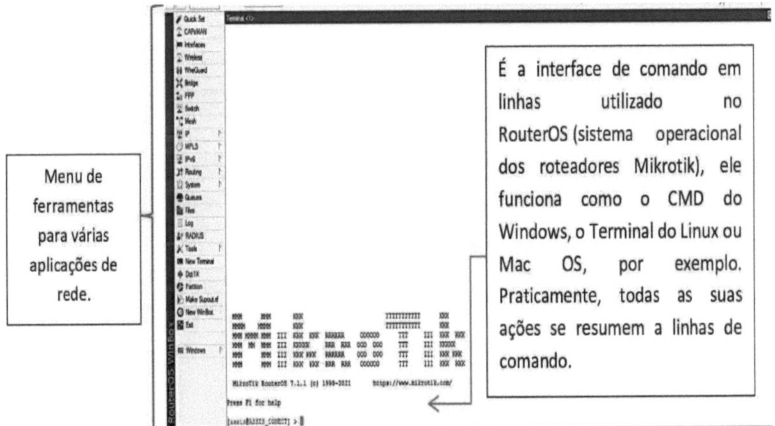

Source: Author (2023).

Mikrotik is an operating system developed in 1997 for routers. It provides great stability, control and flexibility for all types of data and routing interfaces (ROUTERBOARD, 2012). As such, it has various functions such as Proxy, VPN, VLAN, Firewall, Hotspots, QoS and Bandwidth Control (MESQUITA; CABRAL, 2022).

4.1.1 Client A (Via Radio)

The first PING tests were carried out on sunny days, without weather changes such as rain or fog. The customers (A) are served with radio technology and fixed internet plans and are located at the same distances, one has a wide view of the distribution tower and the other does not. Figures 22 and 23 illustrate the test results.

Figure 22 - Customer PING test without a wide view of the distribution tower.

```
Terminal <1>


    MMM      MMM      KKK                          TTTTTTTTTTT   KKK
    MMMM    MMMM      KKK                          TTTTTTTTTTT   KKK
    MMM MMMM MMM  III KKK KKK  RRRRRR   OOOOOO        TTT    III KKK KKK
    MMM  MM  MMM  III KKKKK     RRR RRR OOO OOO       TTT    III KKKKK
    MMM      MMM  III KKK KKK   RRRRRR  OOO OOO       TTT    III KKK KKK
    MMM      MMM  III KKK KKK  RRR RRR  OOOOOO        TTT    III KKK KKK

    MikroTik RouterOS 7.1.1 (c) 1999-2021      https://www.mikrotik.com/

    Press F1 for help



    [assis@ASSIS_CONECT] > ping 172.35.2.248
       SEQ HOST                                   SIZE TTL TIME          STATUS
         0 172.35.2.248                                                 timeout
         1 172.35.2.248                             56  64 11ms723us
         2 172.35.2.248                             56  64 14ms770us
         3 172.35.2.248                             56  64 17ms139us
         4 172.35.2.248                             56  64 3ms495us
         5 172.35.2.248                             56  64 1ms732us
         6 172.35.2.248                             56  64 3ms42us
         7 172.35.2.248                             56  64 4ms792us
         8 172.35.2.248                             56  64 4ms724us
         9 172.35.2.248                                                 timeout
        10 172.35.2.248                                                 timeout
        11 172.35.2.248                             56  64 5ms390us
        12 172.35.2.248                             56  64 2ms44us
        13 172.35.2.248                             56  64 17ms256us
        14 172.35.2.248                             56  64 159ms810us
        15 172.35.2.248                             56  64 179ms725us
        16 172.35.2.248                             56  64 26ms194us
        17 172.35.2.248                                                 timeout
        18 172.35.2.248                             56  64 4ms252us
        19 172.35.2.248                             56  64 147ms304us
        sent=20 received=16 packet-loss=20% min-rtt=1ms732us avg-rtt=37ms712us max-rtt=179ms725us

    [assis@ASSIS_CONECT] >
```

Source: Author (2023).

Figure 22 shows the PING test carried out from the server to the end user identified by the system with IP address 172.35.2.248 (HOST) and being served by radio internet, without a wide view of the distribution tower.

The Mikrotik terminal command lines (SEQ) from 0 to 19 respond to the round-trip information of the data packets sent to the host in (ms) milliseconds. On lines 0, 8, 9 and 17, the response expressed is *timeout,* which represents the delay in communication between the user and the terminal, with failures occurring between them. We can say that the internet connection will be unstable, and the transmission of audio or video data in real time (*streaming*) will be affected.

Figure 23 - PING test - with a wide view of the tower.

```
Terminal <1>


   MMM        MMM      KKK                                TTTTTTTTTTT      KKK
   MMMM       MMMM     KKK                                TTTTTTTTTTT      KKK
   MMM MMMM MMM III KKK KKK  RRRRRR    000000      TTT    III KKK KKK
   MMM  MM  MMM III KKKKK    RRR RRR  000  000     TTT    III KKKKK
   MMM       MMM III KKK KKK  RRRRRR  000  000     TTT    III KKK KKK
   MMM       MMM III KKK KKK  RRR RRR  000000      TTT    III KKK KKK

   MikroTik RouterOS 7.1.1 (c) 1999-2021      https://www.mikrotik.com/

 Press F1 for help



 [assis@ASSIS_CONECT] > ping 172.35.2.163
   SEQ HOST                                    SIZE TTL TIME          STATUS
     0 172.35.2.163                              56  64 4ms364us
     1 172.35.2.163                              56  64 20ms738us
     2 172.35.2.163                              56  64 61ms162us
     3 172.35.2.163                              56  64 58ms272us
     4 172.35.2.163                              56  64 42ms743us
     5 172.35.2.163                              56  64 59ms187us
     6 172.35.2.163                              56  64 13ms986us
     7 172.35.2.163                              56  64 11ms222us
     8 172.35.2.163                              56  64 5ms841us
     9 172.35.2.163                              56  64 64ms690us
    10 172.35.2.163                              56  64 25ms470us
    11 172.35.2.163                              56  64 29ms625us
    12 172.35.2.163                              56  64 5ms793us
    13 172.35.2.163                              56  64 4ms750us
    14 172.35.2.163                              56  64 70ms595us
    15 172.35.2.163                              56  64 38ms472us
    16 172.35.2.163                              56  64 12ms615us
    17 172.35.2.163                              56  64 62ms273us
    18 172.35.2.163                              56  64 36ms745us
    19 172.35.2.163                              56  64 23ms751us
     sent=20 received=20 packet-loss=0% min-rtt=4ms364us avg-rtt=32ms614us max-rtt=70ms595us

 [assis@ASSIS_CONECT] >
```

Source: Author (2023).

Figure 23 shows the PING test carried out from the server to the end user identified by the system with IP address 172.35.2.163 (HOST) and being served by radio internet, with a wide view of the distribution tower.

In this PING test, the data sent from the server to the host was unchanged, i.e. the Mikrotik terminal command lines did not respond to the expression *timeout,* all responses were in (ms). No communication failures are occurring between them, contributing to a more stable internet.

4.1.2   Customer B (Optical Fiber)

Customers served by optical fiber do not suffer from external interference and have no problems with obstructions or weather variations. The following cases are at different distances from the distribution server. Figures 24 and 25 illustrate the PING test carried out on fiber users.

Figure 24 - PING test user optical fiber near the server

```
Terminal <1>


    MMM        MMM        KKK                                TTTTTTTTTTT        KKK
    MMMM       MMMM       KKK                                TTTTTTTTTTT        KKK
    MMM MMMM MMM   III    KKK  KKK   RRRRRR      OOOOOO          TTT     III   KKK  KKK
    MMM  MM  MMM   III    KKKKK       RRR  RRR   OOO  OOO        TTT     III   KKKKK
    MMM      MMM   III    KKK KKK    RRRRRR      OOO  OOO        TTT     III   KKK KKK
    MMM      MMM   III    KKK  KKK   RRR  RRR    OOOOOO          TTT     III   KKK  KKK

    MikroTik RouterOS 7.1.1 (c) 1999-2021        https://www.mikrotik.com/

Press F1 for help


[assis@ASSIS_CONECT] > ping 172.35.2.251
  SEQ HOST                                      SIZE TTL TIME        STATUS
    0 172.35.2.251                                56  64 912us
    1 172.35.2.251                                56  64 697us
    2 172.35.2.251                                56  64 1ms68us
    3 172.35.2.251                                56  64 920us
    4 172.35.2.251                                56  64 965us
    5 172.35.2.251                                56  64 1ms229us
    6 172.35.2.251                                56  64 1ms407us
    7 172.35.2.251                                56  64 761us
    8 172.35.2.251                                56  64 1ms399us
    9 172.35.2.251                                56  64 1ms436us
   10 172.35.2.251                                56  64 673us
   11 172.35.2.251                                56  64 1ms135us
   12 172.35.2.251                                56  64 871us
   13 172.35.2.251                                56  64 716us
   14 172.35.2.251                                56  64 1ms553us
   15 172.35.2.251                                56  64 1ms235us
   16 172.35.2.251                                56  64 673us
   17 172.35.2.251                                56  64 1ms
   18 172.35.2.251                                56  64 1ms264us
   19 172.35.2.251                                56  64 1ms186us
    sent=20 received=20 packet-loss=0% min-rtt=673us avg-rtt=1ms55us max-rtt=1ms553us

[assis@ASSIS_CONECT] >
```

Source: Author (2023)

Figure 25 - PING test user optical fiber far from the server

```
MMM        MMM        KKK                                 TTTTTTTTTTT     KKK
MMMM       MMMM       KKK                                 TTTTTTTTTTT     KKK
MMM MMMM MMM   III    KKK  KKK   RRRRRR      OOOOOO          TTT    III   KKK  KKK
MMM  MM  MMM   III    KKKKK       RRR  RRR   OOO  OOO         TTT    III   KKKKK
MMM       MMM  III    KKK KKK    RRRRRR      OOO  OOO         TTT    III   KKK KKK
MMM       MMM  III    KKK  KKK   RRR  RRR    OOOOOO          TTT    III   KKK  KKK

MikroTik RouterOS 7.1.1 (c) 1999-2021       https://www.mikrotik.com/

Press F1 for help


[assis@ASSIS_CONECT] > ping 172.35.2.155
  SEQ HOST                                      SIZE TTL TIME          STATUS
    0 172.35.2.155                               56  64  967us
    1 172.35.2.155                               56  64  1ms100us
    2 172.35.2.155                               56  64  1ms446us
    3 172.35.2.155                               56  64  764us
    4 172.35.2.155                               56  64  887us
    5 172.35.2.155                               56  64  1ms52us
    6 172.35.2.155                               56  64  1ms182us
    7 172.35.2.155                               56  64  707us
    8 172.35.2.155                               56  64  970us
    9 172.35.2.155                               56  64  739us
   10 172.35.2.155                               56  64  1ms206us
   11 172.35.2.155                               56  64  1ms290us
   12 172.35.2.155                               56  64  1ms12us
   13 172.35.2.155                               56  64  906us
   14 172.35.2.155                               56  64  727us
   15 172.35.2.155                               56  64  1ms303us
   16 172.35.2.155                               56  64  1ms233us
   17 172.35.2.155                               56  64  1ms551us
   18 172.35.2.155                               56  64  841us
   19 172.35.2.155                               56  64  1ms327us
    sent=20 received=20 packet-loss=0% min-rtt=707us avg-rtt=1ms60us max-rtt=1ms551us

[assis@ASSIS_CONECT] >
```

Source: Author (2023).

In Figures 24 and 25 the users are identified with IPs 172.35.2.251 and 172.35.2.155. Both images depict a stable scenario as there are no communication failures and the response in (ms) is much lower than in the radio user tests. The lowest response times were achieved in the fiber optic tests, which is an advantage over radio, since the lower the (ms), the better the internet.

For a better view of the PING results for customers A and B, they are summarized in Table 1.

Table 1 - Summary of PING results Clients A (Radio) and B (Fiber).

CLIENTS Radio(A) / Fiber(B)	sent	received	packet- loss	min-rtt (minimum round trip time)	max-rtt (maximum round trip time)	avg-rtt (average round trip)
Customer A (targeted)	20	16	20%	1ms73us	179ms725us	37ms712us
Client A (no targeting)	20	20	0%	4ms36us	70ms595us	32ms614us
Client B (near the server)	20	20	0%	673us	1ms553us	1ms55us
Client B (far from the server)	20	20	0%	707us	1ms551us	1ms60us

Source: Author (2023).

In Table 1, the PING comparison between the two technologies shows the summary of the PING analysis carried out on the mikrotik terminal, which resulted in the following:

✓ Client A, via radio, had 20% packet loss, and the maximum round-trip time (latency) in the test was 179 ms, which means that browsing the Internet, making video calls, playing online games and *downloading/uploading* media files will take longer than expected. When the packet is not delivered, the PING response is *timeout,* which represents time exhausted (packet loss), affecting internet browsing.

4.1.3 Speed

Internet speed is bandwidth, the amount of data that can be sent to a given user. If a customer takes out a 10 Mbps plan, they will receive up to 10 megs of data per second.

In radio, internet speed can be impaired in the following situations where obstructions and alignment cause increased latency, directly interfering with speed. In fiber optics, there are some particular cases that can influence the increase in latency, which are: attenuation of the optical cable, cracked fiber and dirt in the connector, for example.

In a rural setting, there are factors that affect the speed of the internet for radio users, such as:

- Tree obstructions;
- Long distances;
- Poorly installed internet antennas;
- Equipment operating on the same frequency;
- Channel width.

Because of these factors, radio transmission loses quality. Optical fiber, on the other hand, doesn't have this kind of problem because it doesn't suffer from external interference.

Although the Internet is delivered to homes via fiber optics, it must be taken into account that the router is the equipment responsible for distributing the connection to the end user, because even though it is delivered via fiber, distribution in homes is done via radio, so this equipment needs to be installed in a strategic location in the house and analyze the best channel so that there is no dispute with other routers or devices nearby.

Figure 26 illustrates channel analysis for routers using Ubiquiti's WiFiman tool.

Figure 26 - Channel analysis in routers.

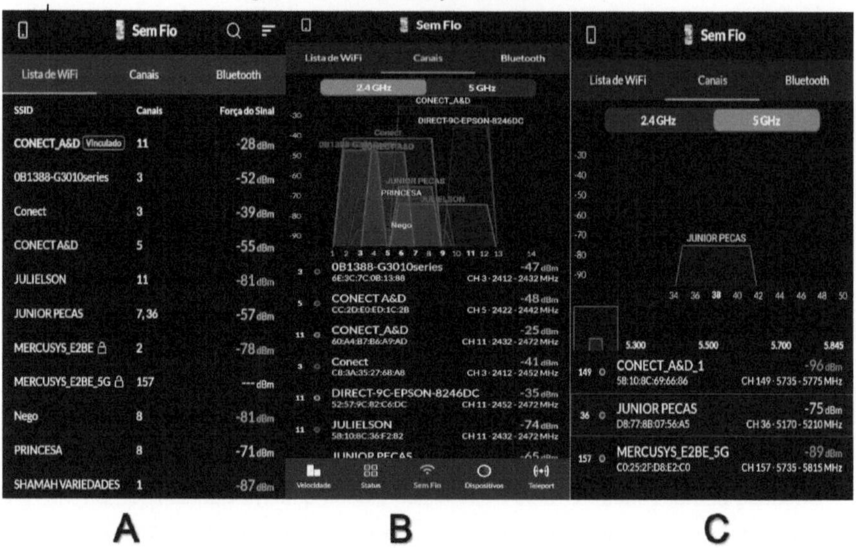

Source: Author (2022).

In Figure 18 there are 3 items analyzed, which are identified below by A, B and C. In item A, which refers to the *WIFI* list, it can be seen that some of the devices connected to the internet are on the same channel, as can be seen: the connect_A&D router and Julielson are on channel 11; Nego and Princesa are on channel 8. This will cause a dispute between these devices which will lead to network instability, connecting and disconnecting end users.

In item B, you can easily identify several channels on the same 2.4GHz frequency, which will cause the internet to malfunction.

Item C emphasizes the 5Ghz frequency, which is an innovation for internet networks, bringing improvements. It was observed that this frequency does not have this problem because there are fewer devices on this network. It is a frequency that supports a higher internet bandwidth, however, the disadvantage is that any obstacles, such as household walls and distances, for example, can disconnect users from the network.

Therefore, the speed of the internet between the two technologies via radio and fiber optics also depends on the proper configuration and installation of the router.

4.2 Analysis of Costs

The investment in radio equipment is cheaper and easier to deploy to serve a certain number of customers, combined with lower cost-benefit and a short-term return. Optical fiber, on the other hand, requires a higher cost-benefit ratio and a long-term return. Tables 2 and 3 show the cost of the equipment for each technology.

Table 2 - Materials and investment costs for fiber optics.

COST OF A FIBER OPTIC NETWORK FOR UP TO 256 USERS			
PRODUCT	QUANT.	V.UNIT	V. TOTAL
AS80-6FO FIBER	4000	R$ 1,60	R$ 6.400,00
SPLITTERS(1X2)	6	R$ 30,00	R$ 180,00
AS80-12FO FIBER	2000	R$ 2,90	R$ 5.800,00
CTOS 1X8	26	R$ 98,00	R$ 2.548,00
CEO	8	R$ 133,80	R$ 1.070,40
SPLITTERS(1X4)	8	R$ 38,00	R$ 304,00
DIO 12 FO	1	R$ 350,00	R$ 350,00
DIELECTRON	200	R$ 5,88	R$ 1.176,00
OPTICAL FIELD CONNECTO7	512	R$ 7,00	R$ 3.584,00
CLOSURES	100	R$ 0,50	R$ 50,00
PREFORMED HANDLES	130	R$ 2,14	R$ 278,20
DROP	20	R$ 490,00	R$ 9.800,00
UN	256	R$ 130,00	R$ 33.280,00
WIFI ROUTER 6	256	R$ 300,00	R$ 76.800,00
FUSIMEC	4	R$ 37,50	R$ 150,00
OLT EPON 256 CUSTOMERS	1	R$ 5.500,00	R$ 5.500,00
GBIC 20 KM EPON	4	R$ 309,36	R$ 1.237,44
BAP	200	R$ 5,02	R$ 1.004,00
LOOK	120	R$ 3,25	R$ 390,00
BOARD M	200	R$ 2,01	R$ 402,00
RB 4011	1	R$ 1.500,00	R$ 1.500,00
GBIC 20 KM EPON	4	R$ 322,39	R$ 1.289,56
MELTING MACHINE	1	R$ 8.000,00	R$ 8.000,00
MAINTENANCE KIT	1	R$ 650,00	R$ 650,00
OTDR	1	R$ 4.000,00	R$ 4.000,00
MAÇARICO AND GAS	1	R$ 120,00	R$ 120,00
EQUIPMENT RACK	1	R$ 350,00	R$ 350,00
TOTAL			R$ 166.213,60

Source: Author (2023)

Table 2 shows the materials and investment costs for optical fiber. The equipment listed is for a network project for up to 256 users. This is characterized as an EPON network.

Table 3 - Materials and radio investment costs.

COST OF A RADIO NETWORK FOR 256 USERS			
PRODUCT	QUANT.	V.UNIT	V. TOTAL
TRANSMISSION TOWER	1	R$ 10.000,00	R$ 10.000,00
SECTOR PANELS	4	R$ .143,19	R$ 4.572,76
RJ 45 CONNECTOR	512	R$ 1,00	R$ 512,00
NETWORK CABLE	12	R$ 399,00	R$ 4.788,00
ROUTERS	256	R$ 80,00	R$ 20.480,00
ANTENNAS FOR HOMES	256	R$ 285,00	R$ 72.960,00
ANTENAS FOR PTP 27dbi	1	R$ 1.500,00	R$ 1.500,00
SWITCH	1	R$ 150,00	R$ 150,00
MAINTENANCE KIT	1	R$ 500,00	R$ 500,00
TOTAL			R$ 115.462,76

Source: Author (2023).

In Table 3 of materials and investment costs for radio, the equipment listed is for a network project for up to 256 users. It was stipulated for the same number of users as in Table 2 in order to compare the costs between them.

In this case, the estimated cost difference is R$50,750.00. There is a noticeable difference in the amount of materials needed to deploy each of the technologies shown in Table 2, which makes radio more accessible for small providers. However, when it comes to performance, stability and greater bandwidth traffic, the ideal is to invest in optical fiber, as this is the trend in data transmission technology.

4.3 Advantages and Disadvantages

The internet is present in people's daily lives, 90% of homes are connected, whether through a computer, cell phone or even *smart* TVs (IBGE, 2022).

As explained in this research, the internet provider in the quilombola community of Umarizal offers this type of service using radio and fiber optic technology. However, knowing the advantages and disadvantages between them is essential. Table 4 lists the characteristics of each technology.

Table 4 - Comparison of the characteristics of the two technologies.

FEATURES	FIBER OPTIC INTERNET	RADIO INTERNET
Connection speed	High download and upload speed of	Speed can be limited by weather conditions and interference
Connection stability	Stable connection e without interruptions.	The connection can be affected byby or electromagnetic interference from objects in the path.
Latency	Low latency, allowing fast response in games online and videoconferences.	High latency, which can result in delays and interruptions during online games and video conferences
Availability	It can be limited in some regions, due to the infrastructure needed to offer this type of service.	It can be available in rural or remote areas where wired internet is not viable.
Price	It can be more expensive than other types of internet connection.	It can be more affordable in de compared to with other types of internet connection.
Technology	It uses fiber optic technology, which allows for high connection speeds and greater stability.	It uses radio frequency technology, which can be affected by electromagnetic interference and weather conditions.

Source: Kassel (2023).

5   CONCLUSION

The provider in the community of Umarizal began its services with radio technology, and experienced the ability to function for years, which at first met the needs of users. However, when demand increased, this technology began to fail in various aspects, which led to the implementation of new fiber optic technology in order to continue meeting the needs of users.

When analyzing the two technologies in operation at the Conect-A&D internet provider in the Quilombola community of Umarizal, mainly by tracing the characteristics of each one, a significant difference in quality and also in the way they operate was clearly seen.

While radio has weak points and some bandwidth limitations, fiber optics transmits a larger bandwidth with low latency, giving more confidence to those who contract the service.

Despite the high cost of laying fiber optic cable, the investment in the new technology brought encouraging results, showing that as it was a better quality service, it was being more widely accepted by the public.

It can be said that, after analyzing the two technologies, it can be seen that fiber optics offers a better quality service, in addition to offering larger bandwidths, but only where there is no fiber optic cable in place does the company offer radio technology.

In this sense, this study also points to a new paradigm to be implemented by the company in the near future: the implementation of a system using optical fiber with the GPON version to later be able to serve users who are still on radio.

The field research showed that both are viable, but radio stands out for its ability to serve users where there are no conditions for laying optical cables.

In order to reach users in more remote places with fiber optic technology, the company's future work also includes the implementation of an underwater optical cable connecting the *link* directly to the city of Baião, as well as the implementation of a DNS server – Cloud Domain Name System.

REFERENCES

ANDRADE, Rosciano Sousa de. **Impact of regulation on the expansion of fixed broadband in Brazil:** a difference-in-differences analysis from 2007 to 2021. 2023. 55 f. Dissertation (Master's Degree) - Master's Degree in Economic Sciences, Center for Applied Social Sciences, Federal University of Rio Grande do Norte, Natal – RN, 2023.

Telecom service balance shows significant growth in broadband. Gov.br. 2022. Available at: < https://www.gov.br/anatel/pt-br> . Accessed on: July 23, 2022.

BOGÉA, Hiroshi. **Between islands, riverbanks and the superb Tocantins, reigns the town of Umarizal - "land of the land".** 1 photo. Available in: <https://www.hiroshibogea.com.br>. Accessed on: August 20, 2022.

BRAZIL. **Law No. 12.965, of April 23, 2014**. Establishes principles, guarantees, rights and duties for the use of the Internet in Brazil. Brasília: Federal Official Gazette,
24 Apr. 2014. Available at: < https://www.planalto.gov.br/>. Accessed on: July 23, 2022.

CORDEIRO, Maurício. **Fiber optic cable**. 21 Dec. 2020. 1 photo. Available at:< https://www.dicasdeinstrumentacao.com>. Accessed on: Aug. 3, 2022.

E.M.E.F DE UMARIZAL (Baião-Pa) (org.). **Report on the village of Umarizal**. Baião: Umarizal School, 2013. 20 p.

FERNANDES, Adriana Orthmann. **IEEE 802.11n**: a study on the new wireless network standard for high performance data transfer. 2009. 152 f. TCC (Graduation) - Information Systems Course, Department of Informatics and Statistics, Federal University of Santa Catarina, Florianópolis-SC, 2009.

FRANCISCATTO, Roberto et al. **Computer Networks**. Frederico Westphalen - RS: Colégio Agrícola de Frederico Westphalen, 2014. 116 p.

FREITAS, Edmar Francisco. **Feasibility study for the deployment of optical fiber**: Capivari de baixo. 2022. 85 f. TCC (Graduation) - Bachelor's Degree in Electrical Engineering, Universidade do Sul de Santa Catarina, Tubarão, 2022.

GERHARDT, Tatiana Engel; SILVEIRA, Denise Tolfo (org.). **Métodos de pesquisa**. Porto Alegre: Editora UFRGS, 2009. 120 p.

IBGE: Internet is present in 90% of the country's homes. **TV Brasil**, [*S. l.*], p. 1-1, 23 Sept. 2022. Available at: <https://tvbrasil.ebc.com.br>. Accessed on: August 20, 2023.

INFOGRAPHIC: **Main differences between EPON and GPON networks**. 20 aug. 2019. 1 photo. 596x1026. Available at:< https://www.fibracem.com>. Accessed on:

23 Aug. 2022.

INTERNET WORLD STATS - **Usage and population statistics**. Available at: <https://www.internetworldstats.com/>. Accessed on: July 21, 2022.

KASSEL, Gabriele Assif. **What's the difference between fiber internet and radio internet?** Available at: <https://ad-freaks.com/qual-a-diferenca-entre-a-internet-fibra-e-internet-via-radio/>. Accessed on: September 25, 2023.

KUROSE, Jim et al. **Computer networks and the Internet**: a top-down approach. 6. ed. São Paulo: Pearson Education do Brasil, 2013. 658 p. Translation: Daniel Vieira; technical review Wagner Luiz Zucchi.

LUYS, Emerson. **Wifi provider structure for those who want to set up a provider**. 19 Apr. 2017. 1 photo. 1280x720. Available at: <www.i7telecom.com.br>. Accessed on: August 3, 2022.

MACEDO, Ricardo Tombesi et al. **Computer networks**. Santa Maria-RS: Federal University of Santa Maria, 2018. 196 p.

MATHEUS, Yuri. **Getting to know some network topologies**. 27 Sep. 2018. 2 photos. Available at: https://www.alura.com.br. Accessed on: Aug. 6, 2023.

MENESES FILHO, Esdras Antonio de. **Sizing a PON FTTH fiber optic network**. 2018. 93 f. TCC (Graduation) - Electrical Engineering Course, Multidisciplinary Center of Caraúbas, Federal Rural University of the Semi-Arid, Caraúbas-RN, 2018.

MESQUITA, Rafael Antônio de; CABRAL, Rafael Hungaro. **SGP - Customer Management System for Internet Service Providers**. 2022. 23 f. TCC (Graduation) - Electrical Engineering Course, Fepesmig, Minas Gerais, 2022.

NEIVA, Paulo Matheus de Souza. **Computer Networks.** 18 Jul. 2013. 1 photo. 452x295. Available at: http://fabrica.ms.senac.br. Accessed on: Aug. 6, 2023.

Influence of covid-19 on internet quality in Brazil. Brazil: Ponto Br Information and Coordination Center (Nic.Br), 2020. 40 p.

NIC.BR. In the Media - **The impact of the pandemic on Internet use**. 7 Apr. 2022. Available at: <https://www.nic.br/noticia/na-midia/cyber-cultura-o-impacto-da-pandemia-no-uso-da-internet/>. Accessed on: July 26, 2022.

POSSEBON, Tainã Vieira. **Internet provider via radio frequency.** 2014. 40 f. TCC (Graduation) - Computer Network Technology Course, Colégio Técnico Industrial, Universidade Federal de Santa Maria, Santa Maria, RS, Brazil, 2014.

PRESCOTT, Roberta . **Internet connection advances (a lot) in rural areas between 2019 and 2021**. 21 Jun. 2022. Available at: < https://www.abranet.org.br/>. Accessed
on: July 25, 2022.

RAMOS, Adriano Pereira; NEVES, Ebert Melo das. **Study of new generation PON network technologies in the FTTX scenario.** 2018. 85 f. TCC (Graduation) - Telecommunications Engineering Course, School of Engineering, Universidade Federal Fluminense, Niterói – RJ, 2018.

RAMOS, Diego Mendes. **The importance of information security in WIFI networks**. 2020. 34 f. TCC (Graduation) - Computer Science Course, School of Exact and Computer Sciences, Pontifical Catholic University of Goiás, Goiânia, 2020.

GPON Network: Passive Optical Networks - PON. Aug. 3, 2023. 1 photo. 510x242. Available at: <https://www.teleco.com.br/>. Accessed on: 8 Aug. 2023.

REIS, Fábio dos. **Network topologies**. 22 Jun. 2016. 4 photos. Available at: http://www.bosontreinamentos.com.br. Accessed on: Aug. 6, 2023.

SILVA, Marco Aurélio da. **Passive optical networks and LAN networks**. 2018. 49 f. Monograph (Specialization) - Specialization Course in Computer Networks and Teleinformatics, Academic Department of Electronics, Federal Technological University of Paraná, Curitiba, 2018.

SOARES, Rafael Marques de Salles; MARTINS, Savio Candido. **RTMP protocol:** a practical project. 2017. 54 f. TCC (Graduation) - Bachelor's Degree in Computer Science, Institute of Science and Technology, Universidade Federal Fluminense, Rio das Ostras, 2017.

Configuration software for use with RouterOS. Available at: <https://winbox.softonic.com.br/>. Accessed on: September 25, 2023.

TANENBAUM, Andrew S. et al. **Computer Networking**. 5. ed. São Paulo: Pearson Prentice Hall, 2011. 600 p. Translated by Daniel Vieira.

VIEIRA, Vinicius de Oliveira. **Mapping the fiber optic internet network of ISP provider wrlink telecom in the municipality of Sousa-PB.** 2017. 105 f. TCC (Graduation) - Administration Course, Center for Legal and Social Sciences, Federal University of Campina Grande, Sousa - PB 2017.
WINBOX. Available at: https://winbox.softonic.com.br/. Accessed on: September 25, 2023.

Printed by Books on Demand GmbH, Norderstedt / Germany